Building Your Lifeplan™

Taking Care of You & Taking Care of Tomorrow

2nd Edition

Timothy W. Caldwell

Renée A. Harvey

Counselors at Law

estateandelderlawgroup.com

Building Your Lifeplan™
Taking Care of You &
Taking Care of Tomorrow

Lifeplan™

ISBN-13: 978-1717200402
ISBN-10: 1717200400

Caldwell Law
Hanover Road Professional Center
367 Route 120, Suite B-6, Lebanon NH 03766
Phone: (603) 643-7577 Toll Free: (877) 643-7577
estateandelderlawgroup.com

*This book is dedicated to our families,
the families we have had the pleasure
of working with,
and to the families we will
work with in the future.*

Disclaimer & Terms of Use

By consulting this guidebook all users understand, acknowledge, and agree to all of the following Disclaimers and Terms of Use.

This entire publication is for discussion and informational purposes only. It is intended to provide general information about some of the law applicable to estate planning and estate settlement. The authors, Caldwell Law, or anyone forwarding or reproducing this work shall have neither liability nor responsibility to any person or entity with respect to any loss or damage caused, or alleged to be caused, directly or indirectly by the information contained in this work.

This work does not represent tax, accounting, or legal advice. Users are advised to consult with, and should rely on, their own advisors. This book is not designed to replace any legal or other professional advice by licensed and qualified advisors.

The information contained in this publication is believed to be accurate. However, laws, circumstances, and several other unknown factors can render any content contained herein to be unreliable, unusable, and/or inaccurate at any time and without notification.

All users assume full responsibility for outcomes and results from application of or reliance on this material. All users accept full responsibility for consulting qualified legal counsel to discuss this material and their own unique legal concerns, issues, and circumstances. The authors, Caldwell Law, publisher, and any affiliates make no offers, promises, warranties, or guarantees of any type to anyone by allowing access to this publication.

Table of Contents

Introduction

Estate planning is about coming to terms with the fact that ultimately we all lose control — either because of incapacity or death — and then doing something about it before it is too late. Our firm's motto, *"Taking Good Care of Tomorrow"* captures the essence of estate planning:

- It is about you (your care, your hopes, your dreams, and your legacy);
- It is about your beneficiaries (how can you best help them?); and
- It is about the process ("estate *planning*" not an "estate plan") because life changes...laws, assets, circumstances, beneficiaries, and your goals all may change as well.

Plans must be reviewed and updated as circumstances, objectives, laws and thinking change. The best way to prepare and plan for change is to be clear on how you want things to work today and tomorrow. Then review your plan periodically to make sure it will still work for you and your beneficiaries. By clarifying your goals, we can help you create a plan to achieve your objectives.

Estate planning cannot be done in isolation. In addition to legal counsel, it requires input from financial and insurance professionals, tax professionals, long-term care, and medical providers. You also need to engage your helpers. *Helpers* is the term we use for agents, executors, and trustees. Helpers are *fiduciaries*. A fiduciary is a person or entity invested with rights, powers, and obligations to be exercised for the benefit of another person(s). It cannot be overemphasized, helpers must be taught (and re-taught) how things are supposed to work—they must be ready for inevitable transitions.

Lastly, it is critically important for your assets to be owned, or "titled," in a manner consistent with the terms of your planning goals. Failure to pay attention to this often overlooked aspect of planning can lead to unintended and sometimes disastrous results.

We will discuss many aspects of planning in this book. We hope it will help you begin to think about your life and what a plan that works for you would look like. Our goal - the reason our office exists - is for all of our clients to be able to answer YES to *our four simple questions*:

1. Do I understand my estate plan?
2. Does it meet my goals and will it have a positive impact on my beneficiaries?
3. Are my assets titled in a manner consistent with my plan?
4. Have I thoroughly informed my helpers of my wishes and kept them up-to-date on changes in my thinking and to my plan? (i.e. Do they know what I want them to do?)

We want to help you to understand the importance of these questions so you can answer YES to all four, with confidence. Finally, as you read this book, it may be helpful to refer to the glossary of some common estate planning terms. (See page 96)

Chapter 1:
Why Create an Estate Plan?

When thinking about planning for your future, it is essential to understand your options in order to prepare for your own needs, as well as to decide what you hope to do for the loved ones you will someday leave behind.

Why Create an Estate Plan? There are multiple reasons and different ways to articulate them. We like Yogi Berra's: "If you don't know where you are going, you'll end up someplace else."

One of the biggest misconceptions we encounter in our practice is the belief that only the very wealthy need to have an estate plan. Few things could be farther from the truth. Everyone can benefit from estate planning, regardless of their financial wealth.

An effective estate plan is really a Lifeplan™. It is your plan to successfully manage current and future financial and health challenges, to meet the needs and wishes you have defined for yourself, and to provide for your family and for your beneficiaries. Our clients ask us to help them create, improve, maintain, and implement their plan to clearly set out their wishes. A Lifeplan™ is designed to take care of you and to take care of tomorrow.

Over the years, we have conducted hundreds of classes to teach people about the issues they must consider when preparing an estate plan. We often start with this question:

"Why prepare an estate plan?"

The most common answers we hear are:

- To have peace of mind
- To assure the efficient transfer of assets to family members
- To get organized and not leave a mess
- To preserve and protect assets from risks such as law suits, remarriage, divorce, and addictions
- To take care of my family
- To support my favorite charities
- To plan for nursing home costs/Medicaid
- To take care of my minor children
- To take care of my disabled children
- To take care of divorcing children or children with addictions
- To minimize taxes
- To avoid probate

What we'd also like to hear is:

"To take care of me if I am unable to care for myself."

When thinking about estate planning, nearly everyone focuses on what happens after they die. This is an important issue. However, focusing exclusively on post-mortem issues misses the most important person in your plan: You.

- How do you want to live?
- Where do you want to live?
- How do you want to be cared for if you are unable to care for yourself?
- How do you want to be cared for if you are unable to make health decisions for yourself?

- What do you want to accomplish in the time left to you?
- Who do you want to reconnect with?
- What relationships do you need to tend to?
- What is really important to you?

Failing to have a plan can have broad implications while you are alive, such as unnecessary guardianship proceedings, missed opportunities to protect assets for yourself and your loved ones, and unnecessary taxation, expenses, and professional fees.

Building a Lifeplan™ is a process. It isn't a "set it and forget it" event. It is an opportunity for you to determine your needs, your goals, your wishes, and to define your legacy. As your and your beneficiaries' life and circumstances evolve, so must your plan. It must be reviewed and updated regularly to assure it is current and will achieve your goals. By its nature, planning leads to questions, conversations, and action.

You develop your Lifeplan™ in three distinct phases, all of which are interconnected:

1. The first phase involves counseling and considering these questions: What can I do? What do I want to do? How do I want things to work today and in the future?
   Ask yourself: What does a plan that works for me look like?

   Goal: Create and understand your plan.

2. Once your plan is created, the next phase is to make sure it continues to reflect your best thinking as your

desires and circumstances change and the needs and circumstances of your beneficiaries change. We recommend the maintenance and improvement process be ongoing throughout your life.

Ask yourself: Does this plan still work for me? Down the road, will this plan still work for me and my people?

Goal: Refresh your understanding of your plan. Make sure it still reflects your goals.

3. The third phase involves transferring your assets and your values to your beneficiaries in a manner that will benefit them.

Ask yourself: Are each of my gifts made in a constructive manner? Will they have a positive impact on my beneficiaries?

Goal: Your bequests enhance your beneficiaries' lives and circumstances and are appreciated.

During each of these phases and any periods in between, our goal is for you to be able to answer YES to all of our four simple questions:

1. Do I understand my estate plan?
2. Does it meet my goals and will it have a positive impact on my beneficiaries?
3. Are my assets titled in a manner consistent with my plan?

4. Have I thoroughly informed my helpers of my wishes and kept them up-to-date on changes in my thinking and to my plan? (i.e. Do they know what I want them to do?)

As you read this book, we hope you will keep these questions in mind. They serve both as goals for creating your Lifeplan™ and as a means to actively review your plan.

In the following chapters, we will describe important issues to consider as you clarify your goals and wishes so you can build a true Lifeplan™ to take care of you and take care of tomorrow.

Chapter 2:
Planning for Incapacity –
Hidden Challenges

As you begin to build your Lifeplan™, you must address the possibility you may lose the capacity to make decisions for yourself. This can be an unsettling thought. However, it is necessary to guarantee your Lifeplan™ is designed to take care of you. Two common goals in planning for incapacity are:

- to make sure things work the way you want them to if you are unable to make decisions yourself;
- to avoid a court proceeding to appoint a guardian over your person or estate.

We are living longer, meaning it is paramount to plan for mental and/or physical incapacity. One cost of longevity is an increased likelihood we may be unable to make decisions for ourselves or care for ourselves.

For example, if we suffer from some form of dementia or otherwise lose our ability to control our lives, who will make decisions for us? What if we cannot live independently? Will we be able to make decisions about the level of assistance we want, or will someone else impose their wishes on us?

These can be difficult questions and they often lead to additional equally challenging questions:

- Will your helpers be able to assist you during a period of incapacity or disability?
- Will your helpers *really* know what you want?

- Will your helpers help you do what you want to do, or will they focus on what they think is best for you or what is easiest for them?
- Will your helpers be able to assist your beneficiaries during your incapacity?
- How will disagreements among your beneficiaries (or helpers) be handled?

In other words, how can you ensure things will be taken care of in the same way they would have been had you remained capable of making the decisions yourself? Can you plan for the inevitable wrinkles in life? Can you create a process to address these potential challenges? Addressing these issues is a critical part of everyone's planning. Ultimately, you must determine how you want things to work during your lifetime and after your death.

Incapacitated has a very specific meaning; it signifies you do not have the mental ability to make competent decisions. Generally speaking, your doctor makes the determination about whether or not you have the capacity to make health care decisions. Frequently, a doctor's decision is sufficient in terms of your ability to make financial decisions as well, but not always. Sometimes a court-led guardianship proceeding is necessary to determine whether or not you have the capacity to make decisions for yourself.

As we age, the risk of mental incapacity increases. According to the Alzheimer's Association, at age sixty-five 1 in 9 people has Alzheimer's. The incidence of the disease increases to 1 in 3 by age eighty-five. This risk, and others, must be planned for so your wishes are known in advance and your helpers are equipped to act on your behalf.

The best way to maintain control over our lives when we suffer from mental incapacity is to decide now who will make medical and other health related decisions for us and who we want to handle our financial affairs if we lose the ability to make them ourselves — and then be clear to those people about your thinking.

Powers of Attorney

There are legal documents we use to help you provide instructions about your preferences. These include an Advance Directive (frequently called a Health Care Power of Attorney or Health Care Proxy) and a General Durable Power of Attorney (sometimes called a Power of Attorney for Financial Matters). You, the Principal, will appoint an agent in each case to act for you.

An Advance Directive is the tool we use to empower a your Health Care Agent to advocate for your preferences and wishes regarding the care of your person including medical treatment. Your Agent may make all health care decisions for you, but only when your doctor determines you are no longer able to make your own health care decisions. An Advance Directive typically includes specific instructions about life sustaining treatment and withdrawing medically administered nutrition and/or hydration.

With many diseases, including Alzheimer's, the instructions you give your Agent may vary as your condition progresses. For instance, you may want certain types of care if your illness is "mild" while you may not want the same level of care if your illness progresses to "moderate" and "severe."

Having an Advance Directive increases the likelihood your health care choices and instructions will be followed. It is a critical tool. However, it alone is not enough. You must have conversations with your Agent, your alternate Agents, and your physician about your wishes. Your primary and alternate Agents must be well-informed about your preferences and be ready to step into your shoes to make sure you receive your desired health care preferences. Do not assume your Agent understands your wishes or what is important to you. Have the conversation, again and again.

Your Agent's authority to act ends at your death or in the event you regain capacity. Reviewing your choices for your care with your Agents and talking to them about your wishes is a critical part of keeping your estate plan up-to-date.

Note: sometimes you may want your Agent to make decisions that are inconsistent with what you instructed in your Advance Directive. Imagine this scenario: you are terminally ill and are expected to die within six months. You have an up-to-date Advance Directive. In it you directed that no extraordinary measures be used to keep you alive. You also really want to go to your granddaughter's graduation in four months. Three months later you suffer a health setback and are unable to make health care decisions for yourself. The medical team looks to your Agent for direction. What is the question your Agent needs to ask? Not whether treatment will make you better, it won't. Rather, the question is whether the treatment is likely to let you attend your granddaughter's graduation in reasonable comfort. In other words, your Agent may make a decision that is inconsistent with the explicit terms of your Advance Directive. Your Agent needs to understand your wishes AND understand what is important to you.

Many married couples assume that in the event of their incapacity, their spouse will have the legal right to make all decisions for them. Parents frequently make the same assumption with respect to their dependent children. Although some states like New Hampshire have adopted Health Care Proxy laws that serve as a default mechanism in the event a person does not have a valid Advance Directive, you should not rely primarily on this kind of statute. In most cases, planning is required and always recommended. The Probate Courts have a growing number of guardianships due to the failure to create effective Health Care and Financial Powers of Attorneys in advance of incapacity.

In addition to an Advance Directive, all estate plans include a General Durable Power of Attorney. This helps ensure your financial affairs are managed and maintained as you wish them to be.

Unless you state otherwise, it is likely your General Power of Attorney will be effective immediately, even while you are still capable of handling your own affairs. It is common for people to sign Powers of Attorneys without knowing this. It is important to carefully consider when you want your Agent to have authority. The decision is yours and, as with all other aspects of your Lifeplan™, the answer and the designation of Agents may change over time.

The Agent under your General Durable Power of Attorney frequently has broad powers to deal with your property and property interests. Common powers include: check writing, investing assets, dealing with digital assets, and paying taxes. Additional powers may be granted such as authority for gifting and the authority to adjust your estate plan in the event of changed circumstances or changes in the law. For instance, Medicaid planning may change and you will need to restructure. We call these powers extraordinary powers.

Not all of our clients wish to give such broad authority. How much power do you want your Agent to have? Careful counselling on these questions is critical. You must understand your options and the potential impact of your decisions.

Another thing to keep in mind is the potential liability of the Agent. This can happen if the Agent misappropriates funds or makes gifts on your behalf when long-term nursing home care is imminent.

As with the Advance Directive, the authority given in a General Durable Power of Attorney ends at death. Frequently Agents use the power post mortem—without knowing it has expired or in an effort to complete unfinished work. A common example is writing checks against the deceased person's account. Sometimes this does not cause harm—but it is not done without authority and it could lead to personal liability to the estate or a creditor of the estate.

Guardianship

If you have signed a General Durable Power of Attorney and an Advance Directive, it is less likely a guardianship will be required if you become mentally incapacitated. However, sometimes a guardianship is necessary, even if you have these tools. For example, someone may have to petition the Probate Court for a guardian in the event that an agent cannot serve or misuses their authority, or if the Principal refuses medical treatment chosen by their agent.

Because a guardianship takes away a person's rights to make some important decisions for themselves, it is an adversarial court proceeding. It is initiated by an "interested person" in the appropriate Probate Court. An attorney is appointed to represent and defend the rights of the proposed ward. Frequently, an attorney represents the person petitioning for the guardianship, the petitioner. If it is proven the "proposed ward" is legally incompetent, the Court will appoint a guardian and grant the authority to make financial and/or personal and health care decisions for the ward.

A guardian's authority can be very broad or it can be limited, depending on the circumstances. Some states permit the nomination of the person(s) you would like to serve as your guardian, if it becomes necessary.

Once a guardian has been appointed, they will be informed of their duties by the Court. The Court will require the guardian to post a bond to ensure the guardian's faithful performance of their duties to the ward. The guardian must conduct an asset search and file an initial inventory soon after being appointed.

In addition, on each anniversary of the guardian's appointment, the guardian must file an account showing all income paid to the ward or earned by the ward's property, all expenses paid on behalf of the ward, and the amount of the ward's assets being held by the guardian. If the guardian has authority over the ward's "person" the guardian will also make health care decisions on behalf of the ward and file an annual report regarding the status of the ward's health.

Review and Update

Who you choose to be your helpers is critical to the success of your plan. It is important to choose carefully and to the extent possible to avoid basing your decisions on the feelings or expectations of others. The oldest son is not always the best choice. Rather, focus on the following: Knowing what I know today, who is in the best position to make health care decisions for me? Who is in the best position to make financial decisions for me? If the people I choose today are unable to serve, who do I want to serve in their place?

We recommend you update your Advance Directive and General Durable Power of Attorney every two to four years. Review your choice of Agent and review the breadth of power you give them. Check with your bank and financial advisor; will they honor the Agent's authority?

Serving as a helper is a big deal. Your choice of helper is also a big deal. As you choose your helpers, it is critical to make sure they are willing *and* able to serve. Then it is your responsibility to be sure your helpers understand your wishes and their responsibilities. A review of these duties and responsibilities often takes place with your lawyer.

Be prepared; the need for action can be unexpected. Recently, one of our clients reported receiving a call from his father that went something like this:

"I'm in the hospital and they are keeping me here for a few nights. Who is going over to take care of your mother...?
You know, your mother can't spend the night alone."

Our client had no idea if the regular person who house sat was available for one or more nights, depending on how the father's recovery progressed. The client later reported that he had spent a day-and-a-half looking for last-minute care for his mother.

Our client learned a lot from the experience. He learned who his parents' care providers were. He arranged for a back-up care provider. He developed a list of his parents' doctors and made sure their medical offices had copies of his parents' Advance Directives. The custodians of his parents' financial assets received copies of their powers of attorney.

As a result of our client's experience we developed what we call the "Helper's Cheat Sheet." It is a common-sense list of important health care providers and other professionals who play an important role in the principal's life. It is designed to help your helper help you. To download a copy of the form, go to www.estateandelderlawgroup.com.

Where Will I live?

Finding an appropriate living arrangement is an important topic for all of us. You need to ask yourself:

- Where am I going to live if I am unable to live independently?
- Do I have the resources to be able to stay at my home by hiring help to come in and provide services for me during the day and/or the night?
- Do I need to make adjustments to the house to accommodate a wheelchair?
- Can I live with one of my children?
- What if I need assisted living services in a facility?

Related to the question of where will we live is the question of "How we will pay for it?"

Chapter 3 discusses paying for the cost of care and qualifying for Medicaid in more detail.

Many of us fail to take appropriate steps to prepare for the possibility that we will be unable to care for ourselves. Starting to think about this phase of life earlier will give you more and better options.

Building a Lifeplan™ to serve your needs and protect your estate for your beneficiaries is a process and a starting point. For some, it may be overwhelming at first. It is why we do all we can to bring clarity and order to the process. We strive to help you build a plan to meet your needs, and if you desire, to preserve and protect your assets so they can be transferred to your beneficiaries in the future.

In the context of your capacity, potential future health care challenges, and your ability to fund future care needs, please review our four simple questions:

1. Do I understand my estate plan?
2. Does it meet my goals and will it have a positive impact on my beneficiaries?
3. Are my assets titled in a manner consistent with my plan?
4. Have I thoroughly informed my helpers of my wishes and kept them up-to-date on changes in my thinking and to my plan? (i.e. Do they know what I want them to do?)

You may discover you cannot answer YES to all four questions. The goal of the Lifeplan™ planning process is to get you to YES on all four questions.

Chapter 3:
Nursing Homes and Medicaid

Finding an appropriate living arrangement and care is important for all of us. Paying for care can be a critical part of planning, both financial and legal.

Ask yourself:

- Where am I going to live if I am unable to live independently?
- Do I have the resources to be able to stay at my home by hiring help to come in and provide services for me during the day and sometimes the night?
- Do I need to make adjustments to my home to accommodate a wheelchair?
- Can I live with one of my children?
- What if I need assisted living services in a facility?

It is one thing to plan for the challenges of managing your affairs if you become mentally incapacitated. It is an entirely different challenge to plan and pay for specialized care that may be required. As proven time and again, the likelihood you will need assisted care warrants planning for those expenses.

This isn't just a concern if you become mentally incapacitated. There are plenty of scenarios where you may be fully capable of managing your affairs but are physically incapable of caring for your own needs. Some of the most common causes may be chronic illness, a stroke, a physical disability, or other mobility issues.

According to the U. S. Department of Health and Human Services, almost 70% of people turning age 65 will need long-term care at some point in their lives. This creates a risk to you and your estate that should be planned for. Living assistance is an important topic for everyone. Some important questions to ponder:

- Do I want to continue to live at home? Is that even possible?
- How can I maintain my independence and autonomy?
- Will my children or other concerned people let me decide what's best for me?
- Where am I going to live if I am unable to live independently?
- Do I have the resources and the right environment to be able to stay in my own home by hiring help to come in and provide services for me during the day and possibly during the night?
- If I need to use a wheelchair at some point, is my current home wheelchair accessible?
- What are my options (such as living with family or a nursing facility) if I require assisted living?

The next important question is:

- How will I pay for any temporary or permanent long-term care and living assistance I may need?

Answering this question could make you queasy. The expected cost of a nursing home or assisted-living facility can easily range from $78,000 – $120,000 per year. Some facilities are even higher. Having around-the-clock care in your own home could cost in excess of $150,000 per year.

Generally speaking, three sources of money may be available to pay for your care:

1. Your own resources, paying out-of-pocket– self-insuring;
2. Long-Term Care (LTC) Insurance purchased prior to the need;
3. Medicaid, the government welfare program designed to pay for the care of people who do not have the resources to pay for their own care.

Self-Insuring is an option for some, but remember, the annual costs will likely range from $100,000 to $150,000. This is every year and will likely increase annually making the option unattainable for many of us.

Purchasing a LTC insurance policy may be a good option for those who cannot self-insure but have sufficient savings or income to pay the insurance premiums. Some of the factors to look for in a LTC insurance policy include:

- Nursing home and home care coverage;
- Sufficient daily payouts ($250.00/day is a good start);
- Low elimination periods (number of days you must be in the nursing home before benefits begin);
- Acceptable duration of benefits (number of years);
- Renewability (make sure it is guaranteed renewable);
- Waiver of premiums;
- Indemnity vs. reimbursement features; and
- Inflation protection.

Benefits under most long-term care insurance plans begin when you are unable to perform 2 of the 6 activities of daily living (ADL). These are:

- Bathing and showering (washing the body);
- Dressing;
- Eating/feeding (including chewing and swallowing);
- Functional mobility (moving from one place to another while performing activities);
- Personal hygiene and grooming (including brushing/combing/styling hair) ;
- Toileting.

LTC insurance has been undergoing significant changes in recent years. Many policies were sold and not as many lapsed as the insurers expected, and interest rates went down. Insurance companies consequently posted losses. There are fewer companies selling good policies now than in the past and the premiums have increased.

An interesting variation on LTC insurance is what is sometimes referred to as a *hybrid* policy. These policies have a life insurance component and a long-term care insurance component. If you need long-term care, there are funds to pay for part or all of your care, depending on your need and the value of the policy you purchased. If there are funds remaining at your death, they are paid to your beneficiaries.

Policies that indemnify you, sometimes referred to *cash* policies, are generally better than reimbursement policies. As soon as the care need arises, you are given cash to spend as you wish—perhaps by hiring a family member to provide needed care. Reimbursement-type policies require submission of expenses and review by the insurance company and are generally not as flexible as the indemnity plans.

Medicare

For those who are unable to self-pay and who do not have any LTC insurance protection, the last resort is to seek government assistance. Some people are surprised to learn Medicare coverage will not cover the cost of long-term care. Medicare does not cover any custodial nursing home care or non-skilled home health care. The only exception to this general rule is when the recipient has had a qualifying visit to a hospital and requires rehabilitation after discharge. Even in cases where Medicare is the initial payer, payments are limited and do not exceed 100 days.

Medicaid

Medicaid is a government program that pays medical costs and long-term care costs. Medicaid is designed as a payor of last resort. To qualify, you must meet strict clinical and financial eligibility requirements.

Clinical Eligibility for Medicaid

Usually, a person is entitled to Medicaid if they need extensive help with at least one ADL (activity of daily living), and/or they have severe cognitive or behavioral issues, or need daily skilled nursing. Due to cuts in the state budgets of both New Hampshire and Vermont, it is becoming more diffi-cult to meet the clinical eligibility test.

Financial Eligibility for Medicaid

Qualifying for Medicaid is even more challenging financially. The rules for qualifying for Medicaid are strict and voluminous.

A married couple may retain countable assets valued up to approximately $123,000 and certain noncountable assets, both described below. In the context of a married couple, the spouse applying for Medicaid benefits is referred to as the Nursing Home Spouse or the Applicant, while the spouse remaining in the home is referred to as the Community Spouse.

For single people the resources a person is permitted to retain are substantially less. One may retain $2,500 in New Hampshire and $2,000 in Vermont. Under current law, Vermont provides a significant exception to the general rule: a single person can keep his or her home provided the equity in the home does not exceed $570,000.

Transfer of Asset Rules – Transfers between spouses are exempt from penalty. With the exception of a few exempt transfers, transfers for less than fair market value (e.g., "gifts") to a non-spouse made during the 5 years prior to applying for Medicaid, called the *look-back period*, will subject the applicant to a penalty. The penalty period is based on the amount the Medicaid applicant gifted during the look-back period, really making it a waiting period.

Countable and Non-countable Assets

Countable:

- Checking and savings accounts
- Stocks and bonds
- Certificates of deposit
- Life insurance, if face value over $1,500
- Real property, other than your primary residence
- Revocable Trusts: all assets titled in a revocable trust will be considered countable for Medicaid purposes.

- Irrevocable Trusts: are countable if: 1) there are any circumstances under which payment of principal can be made to applicant; if income is payable, then it is counted as part of applicant's/married couple's total income; 2) and transfers to the trust occurred within 5 years of application, i.e., during the look-back period.
- Secondary Automobiles: the value of an additional automobile may be excluded if needed for health or self-support reasons.

Non-countable:

- Primary Residence: A married applicant's house, adjoining land, and buildings on the property are excluded if the equity value of the home is $570,000 (Vermont) or $572,000 (New Hampshire) or less, provided it is in the same state in which the individual is applying for coverage.
- Vermont allows a single person to keep up to $570,000 in equity of their home, but in New Hampshire the nursing home resident must prove a likelihood of returning home.
- Applicants may keep their house non-countable if their spouse and dependent or other relative lives there.
- Personal possessions: Items such as furniture, decorations, art, jewelry, clothing, and appliances are excluded.
- Burial Exclusion: The applicant and their spouse can each have an excluded burial fund set aside. In New Hampshire the amount is $1,500 per spouse. In Vermont, each spouse can set aside $10,000 each. Funds must be set aside in a clearly designated account to cover burial or cremation expenses.

- Enhanced Life Estates ("Lady Bird Johnson" or "LBJ" Deeds): A small number of states, including Vermont, permit this type of deed and "transfer." It keeps the applicant's house in their name during their lifetime and permits the applicant to do whatever he or she wants with the property, and the state does not require it to be sold. Under current law, at the applicant's death the house passes to the grantees named in the deed, free of a Medicaid lien.
- Primary motor vehicles: One automobile is excluded regardless of value as long as it is used for transportation of the applicant or a household member. The value of an additional automobile may be excluded if needed for health or self-support reasons.
- Retirement Funds: Retirement funds such as IRAs, 401(k)s, and pensions may be excludable resources if they are being distributed in periodic payments that include a portion of principal. The payments are counted as income in the month received, though this may vary by state.
- Non-marketable Assets: Assets considered inaccessible for one reason or another. For instance, a parcel of real property may be owned by the Medicaid applicant and other people and they may be unwilling to sell the property.
- Trust under Will – Assets held in a Supplemental Needs Trust (SNT) created under the terms of a Will are not countable if the beneficiary of the trust, including the surviving spouse, applies for Medicaid.

Converting Countable to Non-countable Assets and Exempt Transfers

There are some cases where a penalty period will not be assessed for transfers of assets for less than fair-market value.

For example - Transfer of the home:

- The home can be transferred to a spouse, a child under 21, or child who is blind or permanently disabled.
- Siblings can be transferred to if they have both:
    - lived in the house for a year prior to applying for Medicaid; and
    - an equity interest in the home obtained by gift or purchase.
- Children may be transferred to if:
    - the child lived in the house with applicants and provided applicants care for two years prior to applicant entering a nursing home; and
    - the care permitted applicant to live at home instead of a nursing home.

All other assets may be transferred:

- to a spouse;
- to a disabled child or a trust established solely for the benefit of the disabled child;
- to a SNT solely for the benefit of a disabled person under the age of 65.

Some Strategies for Accelerating Medicaid Payment and Gifting Assets

There are several strategies that can accelerate an applicant's qualification for Medicaid. Some of them are reasonably simple while others are extremely technical. The full details of those strategies are beyond the scope of this book. However, here is a list of some of the more common strategies.

- Various types of Medicaid Asset Protection Trusts
- Funeral Trust
- Personal Service Contract

- Income annuity: The purchase of an annuity is permissible by the community spouse so long as:
  - o The state is named as primary beneficiary after the annuitant's death, unless there is a disabled child, in which case the state is contingent beneficiary;
  - o The annuity is irrevocable and non-assignable;
  - o The annuity does not extend beyond the annuitant's life expectancy; and
  - o The payments are in equal amounts with no balloon payments.
- Transfer of assets using a promissory note
- Purchasing exempt assets such as automobiles, paying for home improvements, or purchasing a new home outright
- Investing assets into exempt income-producing property or other trade or business
- Investing in exempt tangible personal property
- Maximize the community spouse minimum resource allowance
- Maximize use of the community spouse minimum monthly maintenance allowance

Estate Recovery

When a Medicaid recipient dies, the state is obligated to recover Medicaid funds that have been paid towards nursing home care. The estate recovery rules are different from state to state and that is certainly the case in New Hampshire and Vermont.

There are specific limits on a state's right to seek recovery. For instance, recovery can never take place during the lifetime of the community spouse. Recovery is only permitted against the estate of the Medicaid recipient, not against the estate of the community spouse.

There are also restrictions on the state's right to place a lien against a home, particularly if a spouse or other protected individual (e.g., a dependent or disabled child) is living there.

In 2005, New Hampshire expanded Medicaid Recovery to include life estates and joint tenancies in real estate and other property. This action allows New Hampshire to seek recovery from other joint owners in the property and remainder beneficiaries for the amount of Medicaid benefits paid on behalf of the deceased Medicaid recipient, up to the value of the Medicaid recipient's ownership interest in the asset immediately prior to death.

The rule does not apply to real property interests established prior to July 1, 2005, or to non-recipients who paid fair market value for an ownership interest at the time the property was acquired.

Treatment of Annuities

As previously noted, purchasing an annuity for the community spouse will not only enhance her income during the time her spouse receives Medicaid, it is also a way to convert a countable asset into a non-countable asset. If the owner of the annuity receives Medicaid, however, the state will have a lien against the balance of the annuity upon annuitant's death.

The most important take-away from this chapter is to realize there is a high likelihood you your family will incur long-term care expenses at some point in the future.

Cost of this care is significant and can deplete your estate. There are limited options for you to mitigate these expenses. The more you do now to prepare for this risk, the better chance you have of receiving the care you need while protecting and retaining your estate for you and your beneficiaries.

Once you have a Lifeplan™ in place that addresses your long-term care risk exposure it is time to review our four simple questions: can you answer YES to each of them?

1. Do I understand my estate plan?
2. Does it meet my goals and will it have a positive impact on my beneficiaries?
3. Are my assets titled in a manner consistent with my plan?
4. Have I thoroughly informed my helpers of my wishes and kept them up-to-date on changes in my thinking and to my plan? (i.e. Do they know what I want them to do?)

Chapter 4:
Transferring Assets at Death

Once you have tackled planning for incapacity and paying for your long term care, you are ready to plan for your beneficiaries. This involves determining the most effective ways to transfer, preserve and protect assets.

Our clients generally create either a *will-based plan* or *trust-based plan*. Predictably, the primary dispositive instrument of a will-based plan is a will while the primary dispositive instrument in atTrust-base plan is a trust. Each plan includes an Advance Directive and durable powers of attorney, among other planning tools.

What can make the above terms confusing is sometimes a will-based plan includes a trust as part of the will, this type of trust is sometimes referred to as a "trust under a will."

There are two primary reasons for creating a trust: the first is process driven. Generally speaking, assets in a trust are easier to manage during one's incapacity and following one's death than assets titled in an individual's name. This is what is often referred to as avoiding probate. The second reason for creating a trust is substantive. As discussed below, a trust can provide asset protection for or from the beneficiary during the term of the trust.

Wills

A will is an estate planning tool that has been used for centuries. It is a legal document signed with certain formalities that must be carefully followed. A will only applies following the death of the testator, the person who created the will. A will nominates an executor, the person later appointed by the court to settle the estate.

A will controls assets titled in your name alone. It does not control jointly-titled assets or assets controlled by beneficiary designations. Permissible beneficiaries of a will are: people, charities and trusts.

Here is a summary of the process for settling the estate of a person who dies with a will-based plan:

- The will is filed with the Probate Court, typically by the person nominated to be executor;
- An executor is appointed by the Court, with New Hampshire appointments currently taking 4-8 weeks to receive;
- Once appointed, the executor prepares an Inventory of the estate assets;
- Probate assets are used to pay the decedent's debts, creditors,and taxes;
- Once all expenses and debts are paid, and the so-called *claims period* (4 months in VT, 6 months in NH, from the date of appointment) has passed, the executor pre-pares a final account for the Court's consideration;
- Once the final account is approved by the Court, the remaining probate assets are distributed to the beneficiaries named in the will.

If everything goes well, we can expect to settle a will-based plan in Vermont within 6-8 months of appointment. The process takes longer in New Hampshire. If everything is in order, it may take 10-12 months from the date of appointment to settle.

Trusts

A trust is an estate planning tool that has gained wide use over the last 40 or so years. It is a legal document that must be signed with certain formalities. A trust appoints a trustee to oversee its administration and provides instructions for the use of trust property over time, often measured by a life or lives. A trust controls assets titled in the name of the trustee and accounts naming the trustee of the trust as the beneficiary, such as a life insurance policy or a retirement account. A trust does not control jointly-titled assets or assets controlled by beneficiary designations, unless the trust is named as beneficiary of the retirement plan or life insurance policy. Permissible beneficiaries of a trust are: individuals, charities, and trusts.

The primary reason people create trusts is to protect assets during the term of the trust. A fully funded trust (meaning all the trustmaker's assets are in her trust) also has the benefit of avoiding probate which, as noted above, can take a long time. The other reason people create trusts is to facilitate the management of assets during the transition from capacity to incapacity.

Here is a summary of the process for settling the estate of a person who died with a fully funded trust-based plan:

- The will, frequently referred to as a *Pour-Over Will*, is filed with Probate Court. Even though typically there is no probate estate, the purpose of the will is to pick up any assets not transferred to the trustee of the trust during life;
- The trustee prepares an Inventory for the beneficiaries of the trust;

- Trust assets to pay the decedent's debts, creditors, and taxes;
- Once all expenses and debts are paid, the trustee prepares a final account for the beneficiaries' consideration;
- If beneficiaries approve the final account, the remaining trust assets are distributed to the beneficiaries named in the trust.

If everything is in order, we can expect to settle a fully funded trust within 2-4 months of the trustmaker's death.

The basic ingredients of a trust are simple:

1. Instructions for the use of the trust property;
2. A trustee(s);
3. Powers granted to the trustee; and
4. Property held by the trustee.

The trustee has 3 basic duties that must be exercised prudently and in the interest of the beneficiaries:

1. Investing trust property;
2. Accounting for trust property, including preparing income tax returns for the trust; and
3. Distributing trust property.

How a trustee invests property will depend on the terms and goals of the trust. For instance, is it a short-term trust designed to protect the trust property during a beneficiary's minority? If yes, then the investments will likely be conservative and made with an eye toward preservation of the assets as opposed to growth. On the other hand, a trustee of a trust meant to last for a while, like the life of the beneficiary, is likely to invest for growth.

Regardless of the term of the trust, it is important for the trustee to have a process for making investment decisions and to follow that process. At a minimum, the trustee should meet with a financial professional - or an advisor to the trustee - annually to review the beneficiary's circumstances, the appropriateness of the investments, and to make adjustments accordingly. We recommend reviews 2 or 3 times a year.

Accounting for trust property is another critical function of the trustee. The trustee is a fiduciary, meaning the trustee is holding trust property for the benefit of the beneficiaries. Even when the trustee is one of the beneficiaries, the trustee has fiduciary duties. One of the reasons is there is always another beneficiary of the trust. In other words, if there are assets left in the trust at the end of the trust's term, they are distributed to someone or something. The next beneficiaries are one or more of the following: individuals, another trust, or a charity.

How does the trustee decide when and for what to make distributions of trust property? Many trusts have guidelines for the trustee to follow, others do not. It all depends on the type of trust we are talking about.

Most trusts we see are Support Trusts, Unitrusts, Purely Discretionary Trusts, and a type of Medicaid Trust, most of which are a variation of a Purely Discretionary Trust.

Support Trusts

The typical Support Trust includes direction to the trustee to make distributions for the health, education and maintenance of the beneficiary. These guidelines are often referred to as *ascertainable standards.*

A beneficiary can enforce his rights to receive distributions for health, education, and maintenance. In other words, the trustee can be made to make distributions for these purposes. This is one of the reasons these terms, described below, must not be used in a trust if the beneficiary is receiving or may apply for needs-based benefits, such as Medicaid or Supplemental Security Income. Including these terms would make the trust property a countable resource for a beneficiary, making the beneficiary lose his eligibility for the benefits.

As used in trust law, ascertainable standards are broadly defined:

- *Health* covers all matters relating to the beneficiary's health: doctor's visits, prescriptions, wheelchairs, ramps, vehicles to carry wheelchairs, home renovations, hospital bills, and nursing home care, to name a few.
- *Education* includes traditional and nontraditional forms of education to qualify for distributions.
- *Maintenance* means "maintaining" one's lifestyle. What was the beneficiary's lifestyle while the person who created the trust was living? In the case of a surviving spouse, maintenance can be a very important provision in a trust.

A *Support Trust* is often created for a surviving spouse or a child where a balance between asset protection and beneficiary access is sought. A married couple typically functions as a financial unit. They often pool their resources and make a life together. The term *maintenance* in a trust created for the benefit of the surviving spouse permits the survivor to use the whole estate including the property left in trust, to maintain his or her lifestyle.

Note: sometimes the trustee is required to consider other assets of the beneficiary *before* making distributions from the trust. This type of language is typically included when the trustmaker seeks to protect the trust property for the remainder beneficiaries as well as for the lifetime beneficiary.

Generally, the standards of health, education and maintenance are appropriate for long-term marriages. However, when the beneficiary is not the survivor of a long-term marriage, and there are children from another relationship(s), then other terms may need to be considered.

Unitrusts

Unitrusts are designed to pay out a certain percentage of the trust corpus every year. The payout is made up of income and sometimes principal as well. A unitrust is like an endowment; it provides a predictable income stream for the beneficiary(ies). This arrangement is typically for life, with a payout to the remainder beneficiary upon the lifetime beneficiary's death. Sometimes this is the children from previous marriages.

If the percentage paid each year is 3.5% or lower, it is reasonably likely a unitrust will preserve its purchasing power over the term of the trust. In other words, if the trust property is prudently invested it will likely keep up with annual distributions, inflation, and administrative costs. These trusts are frequently used for surviving spouses where the survivor is not the parent of the decedent's children.

A unitrust can also be appropriate if you are worried about your beneficiary's lack of retirement planning. It can be used to structure distributions during retirement years to supplement the beneficiary's income. The trust could provide the beneficiary a certain percent of the trust value starting at age 65. When the beneficiary reaches 70 years of age, the annual distributions might increase to 6%. When the beneficiary reaches 75 years of age, distributions increase to 7%, and so on.

The purpose of this type of trust is to provide a steady income stream for the beneficiary during the balance of their life. When providing an ever-increasing percentage of the trust, preservation of assets for remainder beneficiaries is not a primary goal of the trust.

Purely Discretionary Trusts

The most protective trust we can design without going off shore is a purely discretionary trust. In the case of a purely discretionary trust, an independent trustee is given authority to make distributions for any reason. Because there are no standards that may be enforced, there is no duty to make a distribution, although the trustee nonetheless has a duty to act in good faith. Where a beneficiary has a relatively high risk of being sued, or if the beneficiary needs protection from him or herself, a purely discretionary trust is often the best choice.

Supplemental Needs Trust (SNT)

An SNT (also called a *Nursing Home Trust*) may be appropriate when the beneficiary is or may be eligible for need-based benefits. This type of trust is designed to keep the trust assets from being counted in an aid determination. SNTs are designed to permit the trustee to make distributions that supplement the benefits the beneficiary receives from Medicaid without disqualifying him from receiving those benefits.

Recently we settled an estate that called for outright distributions to the decedent's two children. One of the children was independent, had a steady job and was relatively risk-free. The other child had a history of making bad financial decisions, had been bailed out by his parents a couple of times, and was continually on the brink of financial ruin.

When discussing gifts to the children, our client insisted on equality. Funds used to help the financially-challenged child during the parent's life would be equalized at death, but no steps would be taken that treated the children unequally. In other words, because the gift to the financially-independent child would be outright, so would the gift to the other child.

This is a common sentiment: the kids must be treated equally. We understand, but it is important to remember: equal does not necessarily mean equitable. "Equal" can lead to unfortunate results.

In the case described above, following our client's last update, she lost capacity and died. In the meantime, the financially-challenged child filed for bankruptcy. Because the gift to him was outright, his entire inheritance was subject to the claims of the Bankruptcy Court. Had his gift been left in trust, the gift could have been protected and used for his benefit over the term of the trust.

Every time we contemplate making a gift to someone we have to ask: how will this gift be most beneficial to my beneficiary? To answer this question, think about the following:

- Is your beneficiary married? If so, is it their first, second, third marriage? How stable is the marriage?
- Does your beneficiary have children from a former relationship(s)?
- Is your beneficiary disabled or incapacitated, in a bad relationship, in a risky profession, or subject to other liabilities? Does your beneficiary have an addiction?
- Are you comfortable with your beneficiary's ability to manage the gift?
- Do you want your beneficiaries to immediately inherit all of your assets at your death?
- Do your beneficiaries have children?
- What charities have been important to you during your life? What charities do you want to remember at your death?
- Will your or your beneficiary's estate be subject to estate tax? If yes, your estate plan may want to include a *Credit Shelter Trust* or other tax saving techniques.
- Are either you or your spouse not a U.S. citizen? If your spouse is not a US citizen, special steps may need to be taken to minimize estate taxes.

The Decision Makers – Your "Helpers"

We previously noted that agents, executors, and trustees are all fiduciaries. A fiduciary has an obligation to act in the best interest of the principal, the trustmaker, and the beneficiaries. The choice of helper is critical to the success of every plan.

Sometimes one person is best suited to be the health-care agent while another may be better suited to deal with property and financial decisions. Alternates should always be named.

We recommend engaging a third party or professional trustee if your estate is large or complicated, if a family member lacks necessary skills, or if your family relations are strained. An attorney, certified public accountant, or corporate trustee may be appropriate as one of your helpers. For example, a plan may provide that family members make investment decisions while a professional trustee oversees distributions and accounting.

Continually changing circumstances have seen an increasing use of what is sometimes called a "trust protector" where trusts are used. A trust protector is a person authorized to amend the trust after it becomes irrevocable, typically after the trustmaker's death. This gives the trust added post-mortem flexibility.

We have reviewed some of the factors impacting a plan. Please think of your own situation to help you review the unique aspects of your family when designing your plan, choosing your helpers, and protecting yourself and your beneficiaries. Remember, things change. In order for your plan to be effective, it must be structured to allow for flexibility and reviewed. There can be changes in your or your beneficiary's personal and financial circumstances. Tax laws can change as well. Your plan's flexibility will allow for adjustments to preserve your assets and your wishes.

Again, please review our four simple questions:

1. Do I understand my estate plan?
2. Does it meet my goals and will it have a positive impact on my beneficiaries?
3. Are my assets titled in a manner consistent with my plan?
4. Have I thoroughly informed my helpers of my wishes and kept them up-to-date on changes in my thinking and to my plan? (i.e. Do they know what I want them to do?)

Chapter 5:
Looking Ahead -
Providing Flexibility and Protection

In this chapter we will discuss additional considerations to help you prepare for the unexpected and provide for adaptability in your plan. A well-designed estate plan is the result of a team effort. You, your attorney, and your advisors all have a role in the design of your plan. One of the first issues you and your advisors need to consider is who will be your beneficiaries. In other words, who are the individuals, organizations, and the charities you want to benefit from your plan?

If you are married, your spouse will likely be one of your primary beneficiaries, if not the only beneficiary. But what if you signed a pre-nuptial agreement before your marriage? Is your family a blended family? Do you have children or other people you want to make gifts to? What about your favorite organizations and charities? If the answer to any of these questions is "yes," then you must also decide how and when you want to give your beneficiaries their gifts.

There are two ways to make a gift: outright or in trust. An outright gift is just what it sounds like; the gift is made directly to the beneficiary. The beneficiary can use the gift however they choose. An outright gift is the simplest way to transfer your assets and it is sometimes the best way to make a gift.

In other situations, a trust may be a better way to pass your assets to your beneficiaries. The primary reason people create trusts is to protect assets from the time the gift is made—usually upon the death of the grantor—through the term of the trust, typically measured by years or the life of the beneficiary.

Protection from what?

There are several factors and situations that can jeopardize the assets you intend to give to your beneficiaries. These could include: general life risks, business risks, remarriage, divorce, incapacity, addiction, bad decisions, estate taxes at the beneficiary's death, and the costs of long-term care.

Trusts consist of a set of rules for the use and distribution of property over time. Trusts can be very effective planning tools. When goals are clearly defined, and the trust is designed to meet those goals, and the trust has a mechanism to permit flexibility as circumstances change, a trust can protect your beneficiaries and the assets you give them.

However, as with any type of plan, there are both pros and cons to using trusts. There are costs associated with having a trust; it is not free. To be cost-effective, the value (whether in dollars protected or goals achieved) provided by the trust must exceed the cost of maintaining it.

The biggest cost of a trust is the ongoing administrative expense once the gift is made. In our experience, the annual cost of administering a trust typically ranges from .10% to .50% (a tenth of one percent to a half of one percent) of the value of the trust assets. This does not include the cost of investing or maintaining the assets. This is purely the cost of holding assets in trust.

When considering a trust, it may be helpful to think in terms of insuring the property you are giving to your beneficiaries. Is a trust worth the cost of protecting the assets for or from your beneficiary? Everyone who owns a house must consider whether or not to insure the property. Although the risk of loss is slight, every homeowner we know insures her home. This happens because most people are not able to self-insure. Even those who can are often not willing to do so.

The risk of losing an inheritance is much greater than the risk of losing one's home to fire or flooding. Yet most people do not consider making gifts to their beneficiaries in trust, despite the fact that the trust is a form of insurance designed to protect assets from real threats. Perhaps the most common reasons we hear for this are:

"I don't want to reach from the grave."

and

"I want my beneficiaries to do what they want with their gift."

Many people feel this way. We believe common perceptions about trusts are based on misunderstandings of how a trust can be designed.

While trusts are not for everyone, we think it is important for each of us to consider how we want to make gifts to our beneficiaries. Here are six key questions to answer in order to make an informed decision about the benefits of trusts to your Lifeplan™.

1.How can this gift be most beneficial to my beneficiary?
Sometimes the answer is easy, other

times, especially when your beneficiary is currently not in a good place, it is harder. Often it is helpful to ask your beneficiary how they would like to receive the gift. Remember, you can set up different ways for each beneficiary to receive gifts.

2. **What potential risks could interfere with my beneficiary's receipt and enjoyment of the assets?** Here are some situations to consider:

- *What if your surviving spouse remarries?* Are you concerned about what your spouse will do with the assets during the balance of their life? Will they give the assets to their new spouse who may give those assets to their own children? Will they give the assets to your children upon their death? It is impossible to know the answer to these questions. Nonetheless, it is a question all married people must consider and answer.
- *What if your beneficiary's marriage is the problem?* How strong is your child's marriage? Are you worried about the possibility they may get divorced after your death?

Divorce rates are high. Do you want your beneficiary's share of your estate (whether it is your surviving spouse or a child or other beneficiary) subject to the claims of their spouse? Gifting a beneficiary's inheritance in trust rather than outright can help protect the gift from the claims of the beneficiary's spouse in the event of divorce. There is more on this subject in Chapter 6.

- Another risk for beneficiaries could be their own business risks. *Does your beneficiary own a business?* If the answer is yes, are the risks associated with that business worth protecting against? Again, this is a question only you or your beneficiary can answer.

Many businesses are sole proprietorships. Even where a corporate or limited liability company structure has been created, *co-mingling* of assets or a failure to follow corporate rules can lead to *de facto* sole proprietorships. Here, all the business assets, as well as the business owner's personal assets, may be exposed to business risks and creditors. In these cases, receiving an inheritance in trust can help protect it from the risks present every day the beneficiary is "open for business."

3. **What will my beneficiary's estate tax liability be?** Will the gift you intend to give your beneficiary cause an estate tax at their death? This is particularly important when your beneficiary lives in a state with its own estate tax or when your beneficiary is financially successful on their own. While New Hampshire does not have an estate tax, all the other New England states do. There is more on this subject in Chapter 8.

4. **Will my beneficiary be subject to a special circumstance such as being a minor, having a physical or mental disability, or susceptibility to addiction?** Each of these situations present specific considerations. A properly structured trust can help these beneficiaries, too.

In New Hampshire and Vermont, a trust should be established for a minor beneficiary who is likely to receive more than $10,000. Otherwise, a guardianship will be established for that beneficiary. While a guardianship of a minor's estate is a workable safety net, it does not provide the flexibility of a trust.

For example, a guardianship involves the probate court. This adds another layer of administration that is frequently unnecessary. In our experience, especially in New Hampshire, delays are common due to underfunding of the courts.

For many, the most challenging problem with a guardianship is that it ends when the beneficiary reaches 18 years of age. Receiving what could be large sums of property at this age can be detrimental to the beneficiary. While New Hampshire law permits a guardian to petition the court to extend the guardianship to the beneficiary's 24th birthday, there
is nothing about that age (or any age, for that matter) to suggest an outright distribution is in the best interest of the beneficiary.

An interesting aside, after years of helping people plan for their minor children, the age of 25 kept recurring as the age parents of young children thought would be appropriate to distribute the child's inheritance. We wondered about this age, and after time, set it as our default age of majority. One day we asked one of our doctor clients about it. His rather nonchalant response was:

"Oh yeah, there was a big study about the development of the brain a few years ago and it found that 25 was the age when the brain is fully developed for women...for men it's a little later..." But we all knew that!

Sometimes a beneficiary with a physical disability or mental incapacity receives public benefits based on the beneficiary's disability and lack of income and resources. We call these aids *needs-based benefits*. If your beneficiary receives needs-based benefits, you will want to consider making their gift in trust to ensure that the person can continue to receive those benefits.

Addictions also present unique challenges. When an addiction leads to destructive behavior, care should be taken when structuring the gift for a beneficiary. Will the beneficiary be able to constructively and safely manage the gift? Is it foreseeable that an outright gift would lead to poor choices and harm to the beneficiary or others? If there are questions about the addicted beneficiary's ability to manage the gift on their own, a trust should be considered. There is more on this subject in Chapter 7.

****

A few stories may help to illustrate the dilemmas that beneficiaries may encounter or create. After an update meeting several years ago, one of our clients called and reported:

"My daughter told me she's going to leave her husband after her youngest child goes to college. The problem is, I'm not sure I'll live that long. I want to protect her share of my estate in case I die before she gets divorced."

We discussed her circumstances and the amount he was planning to give to her. Our client then updated his will to instruct that his daughter's inheritance would be held in a protective trust in the event he died before her youngest child left for college and before she was divorced.

Our client left the shares for his other children to be distributed outright. Over the next 3-4 years, at update meetings and chance encounters, our client reported little change in his daughter's intentions. Then, last spring, our client visited us again. He had a big smile on his face. Chuckling, he said,

"My daughter is divorced...and I AM ALIVE."

We shared a laugh and then revised his will to provide for an outright distribution to his daughter — she didn't need the protections any more, at least for now.

Another client found herself in a similar situation. She, too, had just participated in an update meeting where we reviewed questions about how to transfer her assets to her four children. Until that meeting each child was scheduled to receive their shares of her estate in a relatively flexible and liberal manner.

After our meeting she called to say that one of her children was considering divorce, and she thought she would like to protect his share of her estate in case she died before the divorce became final. As we had with other clients, we amended her trust to provide the protection she sought. Four months later one of her daughters called and asked:

"... could you do for me what you did for my brother? My mom said it was ok with her. I think I may be getting divorced too."

We then revised our client's trust again and figured we were in good shape.

Two months later we received a call from our client's helper, another child. She reported her mother had unexpectedly died the night before. Both our client's divorcing children's shares of their mother's estate are in as protective a trust as possible. Both inheritances should withstand the litigation currently taking place regarding the division of their marital assets. That's the key: neither of the clients in our two examples wanted the inheritances they planned to give their children to become marital assets and thus subject to a divorcing spouse's claims.

In the aftermath of the Great Recession of 2008 it was all too common for people to lose their jobs and default on debts encumbering assets that had fallen in value. Foreclosures reached new heights in 2009 and 2010. Sometimes the house was lost. Other times the person's entire savings were threatened or lost and bankruptcy protection was sought. This happened to one of our client's children: the bank was foreclosing on the mortgage encumbering his house, the house was worth less than the debt encumbering it and he filed for bankruptcy. And then our client, his mother, died.

Unfortunately, this client had not updated her plan. The outright distribution to her son that seemed appropriate 8 years earlier had not been adjusted. As we helped our deceased client's daughter - her executor - to settle her mother's estate, we watched her write a check for her brother's entire inheritance to his bankruptcy trustee. A relatively simple change to our client's plan providing for trust protections for her son would have changed the result: his bankruptcy would have proceeded and he would still have the use and control of the trust property his mother left him. As it was, he received nothing.

5. **Will my beneficiary need nursing home care?** If so, how will he or she pay for the care? Do you want to protect the beneficiary's gift for the beneficiary's use and later for the use of the beneficiary's children? It is relatively easy to protect assets from the costs of high nursing home care.

You may want to consider making the gift to that beneficiary in a trust designed to provide for the beneficiary, while assuring the trust assets are not counted if the beneficiary applies for needs-based benefits, such as Medicaid, in the future.

6. **Finally, what is my non-financial legacy?** We are all more than our balance sheets. There are stories, there are memories, and there are values that we hold dear and often want to pass from one generation to another. Sometimes the gift is primarily an association. What is your legacy? There is more on this subject in Chapter 10.

One of the most cherished gifts Tim received from his wife's mother is a little nutcracker in the shape of a dog. In fact, he didn't know what it was when his wife brought it home. He remembers his wife looking at him as if he were an idiot. She reminded him that it was the object her mom put outside the door of her apartment in the assisted living facility every morning to indicate she was up and moving about her apartment—a sign that she was okay. This little dog now sits on their mantelpiece and every time Tim sees it, he smiles and remembers the wonderful relationship he had with his mother-in-law.

For Renée, her father's 1970's green tennis shirt embodies him. It hangs in a shadow box amongst cherished family photos. The shirt is a reminder of the father he was to her, and how much he still means to her family, friends, and the communities he loved. It brings a smile to everyone's face when they see it, and inevitably results in a story being told about him.

We have presented many situations and challenges to consider as you prepare your plan for you and your beneficiaries. The key to a successful plan is to look ahead and plan for the potential issues that could arise, and to provide for flexibility, so both you and your helpers can make adjustments to protect you, your beneficiaries and the assets in your estate.

And as always, it is time again to review our four simple questions:

1. Do I understand my estate plan?
2. Does it meet my goals and will it have a positive impact on my beneficiaries?
3. Are my assets titled in a manner consistent with my plan?
4. Have I thoroughly informed my helpers of my wishes and kept them up-to-date on changes in my thinking and to my plan? (i.e. Do they know what I want them to do?)

In the next chapter we will give you some insight on the unique challenges presented by remarriages and blended families.

Chapter 6:
Blended Families and Remarriage of a Surviving Spouse (This Ain't the Brady Bunch)

Planning for a couple, whether married or not, always raises these important questions:

- "How do you want to care for your surviving spouse/partner?"

- "Are there consequences to your surviving spouse's use of the assets you have accumulated together, or alone, if the survivor of you remarries?"

We cannot answer these questions for you.

While it may be nice to imagine your family relationships will remain as they are during your lifetime, it is more realistic to assume that following your death there will be changes. Here is where things can get a little tricky. In order to increase the likelihood your beneficiaries will receive what you wish for them, you may want to structure your estate so your goals are more likely to be achieved, rather than simply hoping things will work out and be executed as you think they will.

Some facts:

- 80% of men die while married
- 20% of women die while married

While men are more likely to predecease their spouse, when a man is the surviving spouse, he is more slightly more likely to get remarried than a woman who is a surviving spouse. Add to this the new reality of many "blended families."

Some more facts:

- The divorce rate is in excess of 50%
- 75% of individuals remarry after divorce
- 74% of women remarry after divorce
- 80% of men remarry after divorce
- 12% of women have been married twice
- 13% of men have been married twice
- For almost every couple, there will be a surviving spouse

As a consequence, the number of blended families is rapidly growing. What is a blended family? We refer to blended families as families that have children – some or all of whom – are not the children of both spouses – like the "Brady Bunch."

When comparing blended families to traditional families, it is common to find a greater disparity in the age of the spouses and in the ages of the children. Both can create planning challenges. Bringing two families together can sometimes lead to animosity between spouse and stepchildren, among stepchildren, and between parent and children—this can prevent and hinder communication.

And yet, effective communication is key to identifying potential issues and creating a sound estate plan for the unique needs of a blended family. The biggest mistake in blended family planning is not planning for what is unique about the blended family.

A strategy that would work best for your situation may not be obvious. Before you can create a plan you must first think about possible scenarios and then build your plan accordingly. There are many planning tools available. The key is understanding and clarifying your goals and then using the tools that will best implement them.

Here are some common concerns:

- Will my surviving spouse take care of my kids after my death?
- Will my second spouse treat my children fairly?
- What if my surviving spouse gives all of my assets to their new spouse when they dies?
- What if my surviving spouse remarries and then gets divorced? How can I protect my share of our estate from being claimed by the new spouse?

Here's a common situation: If you remarry, you may want to create a trust that will provide for your second spouse following your death and then at the death of your spouse, passes the remaining assets to your children. This can prevent your second spouse from diverting assets from your children. In this way you can care for both your spouse and children.

The more marriages and remarriages, the more children tend to come in to the picture and planning becomes more and more challenging.

Then there is the "Brady Bunch" family where two sets of minor children are joined by their parents' remarriage as a blended family. You and your new spouse need to build a plan that maps out your wishes in case of multiple scenarios – especially when minor children are involved. What will happen if you die while the children are still minors? What will happen if your spouse dies while the children are still minors? And what influence and involvement will there be from prior and future spouses? How can prior and future spouses influence matters?

It may be difficult and challenging to envision all of the *what-if* scenarios that could wreak havoc on the joy of new relationships. However, being realistic and clear-minded is vital to planning in these situations. Ignoring the tough questions rarely leads to good results. Likewise, leaving it up to the survivor of you usually results in what our clients refer to as "the assets going sideways."

It is also very important for you to realize that how your assets are titled will have a significant impact on how your assets are distributed. We cover titling in greater detail in Chapter 9.

A couple of effective and reasonably common planning scenarios for a surviving spouse, especially when the survivor is not the parent of your children, is to give the survivor an income stream from a trust, such as 3-4% of the trust corpus for life. This can help assure the survivor has sufficient income. The plan also has high likelihood of providing for your children at your surviving spouse's death. These trusts can be funded with a variety of assets. Funding them with an IRA or other qualified asset and adding a charitable component can expand your planning opportunities in interesting and often very rewarding ways, and help provide for all your beneficiaries.

The key take-away here is for you to realize divorce, remarriage, and children from other relationships can present some big challenges in estate planning. They are not insurmountable, but you need to anticipate and plan for them.

The more clarity you have about who you want to be your beneficiaries and what you want them to receive and when you want them to receive it – the better chance we can help you structure the plan to deliver on your wishes.

It is especially important that after you planned for these unique challenges you can answer YES to our four simple questions:

1. Do I understand my estate plan?
2. Does it meet my goals and will it have a positive impact on my beneficiaries?
3. Are my assets titled in a manner consistent with my plan?
4. Have I thoroughly informed my helpers of my wishes and kept them up-to-date on changes in my thinking and to my plan? (i.e. Do they know what I want them to do?)

Chapter 7:
"Special" Beneficiaries

Estate planning considerations for Special Beneficiaries include: protecting eligibility for government benefits; providing a framework for the care and management of assets; protecting assets from creditors and predators; extending the life of assets; and providing for a higher quality of life.

Individuals with special needs often face more quality of life challenges compared to those without special needs. Many times, individuals with special needs require added services to meet those needs. The added financial burden often leads individuals with special needs to depend on public benefits to help them meet those costs. Unfortunately, public benefits often fail to meet all of the needs of a disabled individual. The additional needs of those individuals (meaning needs not covered by public benefits) can be met by using funds held in a Supplemental Needs Trust (SNT). Benefits based on financial need include:

- Supplemental Security Income (SSI)
- Medicaid
- Food stamps, cash assistance, utility payment assistance
- Housing subsidies (HUD or Section VIII)

Benefits not based on financial need include:

- Social Security Retirement Insurance
- Social Security Disability Insurance (SSDI)
- Medicare
- Special Education

An SNT is a trust established for an individual with special needs who is or may become dependent on public benefits. The trust is specifically constructed to meet certain supplemental needs and to enhance the quality of life for the beneficiary, the special needs person. Most importantly, the SNT is created so as to not disqualify the beneficiary for the public benefits being received.

The trust property is available for the benefit of the beneficiary in order to provide him or her with goods or services not provided by public benefits programs. For example, SNT funds may be used for in-home care services that would otherwise not be affordable for the beneficiary. If a person with special needs receives these funds outright she may become ineligible for the public benefits. Reinstatement of the benefits can be a difficult process.

There are two types of SNTs: A first-party SNT and a third-party SNT. A first-party, self-settled SNT is funded with assets belonging to the individual with special needs. A third-party SNT is funded with assets belonging to someone else.

A self-settled SNT is often used in the case of a litigation settlement. One example involves an individual who was in a car accident and sued the at-fault driver successfully. By the time the lawsuit settlement was reached, the individual had been declared disabled. Instead of the settlement funds being given outright to the person who is now disabled, they could be placed into a self-settled SNT for the benefit of the individual. This allows the person with the disability to continue to receive benefits and have the settlement money available to him or her for supplemental purposes, increasing his or her quality of life.

Self-settled SNTs have been recognized by federal law since 1993. A self-settled SNT contains a mandatory payback provision, requiring that upon the death of the beneficiary, the State will be paid back from the remaining trust assets up to the amount of public benefits expended on behalf of the beneficiary during his or her lifetime.

Third-party SNTs are similar to First-party SNTs with three critical differences: the trust is created by a third party, the assets transferred to the trust were never the beneficiary's, and there is no pay back provision at the beneficiary's death—the remaining assets can be distributed to other beneficiaries at that time.

Pooled trusts are available for persons over age 65, and usually in long-term care Medicaid cases. These types of trusts are an affordable option when assets are modest. Once transferred assets are not counted as an asset for Medicaid purposes. The assets are managed by a non-profit organization, and the money is used for the needs of the person. There is a payback provision to the State if Medicaid benefits have been provided. In the event there is no Medicaid payback, the remaining trust assets may be payable to the individual's named beneficiaries under the pooled trust.

As with all trusts an individual or corporate trustee is appointed to manage the trust funds. Choosing the right trustee is an important decision: the trustee will be responsible for managing and investing trust assets, and is responsible for following the guidelines regarding proper distributions from the trust. Failing to do so could result in a loss of benefits for the beneficiary.

Managing assets properly is not as easy as it may sound. It is important for the trustee to seek competent advice when needed. There are many roadblocks that can arise in the administration of an SNT, so it is imperative that you have a trustee familiar with the regulations concerning public benefits and SNTs.

As these unique needs are addressed in your plan, remember our four simple questions that we help our clients to answer YES to:

1. Do I understand my estate plan?
2. Does it meet my goals and will it have a positive impact on my beneficiaries?
3. Are my assets titled in a manner consistent with my plan?
4. Have I thoroughly informed my helpers of my wishes and kept them up-to-date on changes in my thinking and to my plan? (i.e. Do they know what I want them to do?)

Chapter 8:
Taxes

After President Obama signed the American Taxpayer Relief Act of 2012 (ATRA) and more recently after President Trump signed the Tax Cuts and Jobs Act (TCJA) tax planning, at least at the federal level, has focused primarily on income tax planning, not transfer tax (estate and gift taxes) planning. Some important provisions of the TCJA expire at the end of 2025. Thus it is likely we will see additional changes to the tax landscape in the coming years.

Understanding the impact of both federal and state income and transfer taxes is important when structuring an effective estate plan designed for asset preservation. Here are the taxes you need to be aware of:

Federal Estate Tax

The federal estate tax, sometimes referred to as a transfer tax, is a unified tax. If implicated, it applies to transfers made during life (the gift tax and generation-skipping transfer tax (GSTT)) and to transfers made at death (the estate tax and the GSTT). Each tax has exemptions or deductions which are summarized here.

Unlimited Marital Deduction

All married couples are entitled to the unlimited marital deduction. The unlimited marital deduction, just as it sounds, really is unlimited. Whatever is transferred to a spouse, is deducted from a decedent's estate and not taxed. Interestingly, this deduction formed the basis of the New York case, <u>United States v. Windsor,</u> in which the U.S. Supreme

Court held that the federal government's heterosexual-only definition of marriage under the Defense of Marriage Act (DOMA) was unconstitutional.

Applicable Exclusion Amount (Exemption Equivalent)

All of us, married or single, are entitled to the federal applicable exclusion. The 2019 limit is $11,400,000, indexed for inflation.

Most of us are not affected by the federal estate tax. In fact, for 2018, less than .1% of estates will have paid a federal estate tax. The tax on the amount over the exemption equivalent is a hefty 40%.

Generation-Skipping Transfer Tax (GSTT)

All of us, married or single, are entitled to an exemption from the GSTT. The GSTT applies to lifetime and testamentary transfers. The exempt amount is indexed for inflation. In 2019 it, like the estate tax exemption, is $11,400,000.

This tax applies to transfers that skip a generation. Perhaps the easiest way to think of a skip is transfer from a grandparent to a grandchild. The GSTT is also implicated when a transfer is made to a trust for the benefit of a beneficiary and then, at the beneficiary's death, the assets are transferred to a person (or to a trust for the benefit of a person) a generation below the beneficiary. The tax on the amount over the exempt amount is 40%. Families work hard to avoid the imposition of the GSTT because it is applied to assets that have already been subject to the estate tax.

Portability

ATRA made permanent the concept of Portability. Portability permits the transfer of the unused portion of a deceased spouse's exemption equivalent to the surviving spouse. The deceased spousal unused exclusion (DSUE) can be applied to future gifts made during the life or at the death of the surviving spouse. To take advantage of Portability and DSUE an estate tax return (IRS Form 706) must be filed in a timely manner.

Portability is a significant benefit for wealthy married couples. For example: If the husband dies and leaves everything to his wife under the unlimited marital deduction, his exemption is unused. Portability permits his DSUE to be transferred to his surviving spouse, thereby doubling the amount of her estate's allowable exemption upon death.

An important note about Portability: It does not apply to the GSTT. Thus families planning for children and grandchildren (or their equivalent from a generational perspective) need to utilize their GSTT exemption at death. They cannot rely on Portability.

Gift Tax

Gift taxes apply to gifts made during a lifetime, but only to gifts in excess of the annual gift tax exclusion, currently $15,000, and only if the aggregate of our life time gifts made in excess of the annual exclusion exceed $11, 400,000 as indexed for inflation. Note: if gifts in excess of the annual exclusion are made, a gift tax return (IRS Form 709) is required. It records the amount of the gifts made during a given year in excess of the annual exclusion. They are accounted for at the donor's death when the estate tax is calculated.

State Estate Taxes

Approximately 20 states have state estate taxes. All New England states, except for New Hampshire have a state estate tax. Massachusetts' exception is $1,000,000, Maine's is $5,700,000, and Vermont's is $2,750,000. Vermont's will increase to $4,250,000 on January 1, 2020 and to $5,000,000 on January 1, 2021.

An important consideration when contemplating gifts to a beneficiary is whether or not the gift, when combined with the beneficiary's own assets, will create a taxable estate for the beneficiary. Gifts to a beneficiary in a trust can prevent the gift from being included in the beneficiary's estate, thus avoiding an estate tax at the beneficiary's death.

Another Estate Tax Issue

A New Hampshire estate not subject to the Federal Estate Tax, but which owns real property in a state that has a state estate tax may be subject to a state estate tax in the state where the real property is located. For instance, imagine a New Hampshire resident with an estate of $3,500,000, which includes a $250,000 cottage on a lake in Vermont. Without careful planning, the New Hampshire resident's estate will be subject to a Vermont estate tax on the value of the Vermont real estate because the total estate would be subject to an estate tax in Vermont (under the current Vermont estate tax law). In that case, Vermont will tax the Vermont real estate as if the decedent had been a Vermont resident.

Here is an overview of the estate taxes and exemptions:

- Unlimited Marital Deduction (only married people can use it)
- $11,400,000 Exemption Equivalent (indexed for inflation)

- 40% tax rate
- Portability (deceased spouse's unused exemption may be used by survivor, with certain exceptions and limitations)
- Gift and Generation-Skipping Transfer Tax Exemption (same exemptions and rates as the estate tax)
- States with estate taxes: CT, DC, HI, IL, MA, MD, ME, MN, NY, OR, RI, VT, WA (tax rates from 8%-20%).

Income Taxes

As the federal estate tax exemption has ballooned from $1,500,000 ten years ago to $11,400,000 million today, the need for estate tax planning has decreased. Today, the income tax is commonly the most important tax to plan for, and in estate planning, leveraging the *step-up in basis*, discussed below, is particularly important.

In its simplest form, income-tax basis is the cost of an asset. The basis of an asset must be tracked because when an asset is sold, income-tax liability, in the form of capital gain, is calculated by subtracting the basis from the sales price. If the sales price is higher than the basis, the taxpayer must report a capital gain, if the sales price is less than the basis, the taxpayer reports a capital loss.

Basis plays an important role in estate planning in two ways:

1. *Basis and lifetime transfers*: When an asset is gifted during life, the recipient of the gift receives the donor's basis in the asset. This is referred to as carry-over basis. If the donee sells the gifted asset, she must look to the donor's basis in the asset given to her to determine whether or not there will be capital gain.

2. *Basis and transfers after death*: When an asset is transferred after death, the beneficiary's basis in the asset is the fair market value on the date of the transferor's death. This is referred to as *stepped-up basis*. In this case, if the beneficiary then sells the gifted asset, she will use the new, stepped-up basis to determine if a tax will be due.

Today many estate plans contain irrevocable trusts that will continue for the benefit of a surviving spouse and thereafter for the benefit of one or more further generations. With these plans it is common for trust assets not to be included in the beneficiary's estate. This will likely create income tax liability when the asset is sold because it will not receive another step-up in basis at the lifetime beneficiary's death.

Drafting trusts to include provisions to work around this potential income-tax trap is an increasingly important aspect of planning. As counterintuitive as it may seem, restructuring (or revising) irrevocable trusts to take advantage of the step-up in basis rules has become an important part of estate planning.

The other common income tax we frequently work to minimize relates to qualified assets such as Individual Retirement Accounts (IRAs), 401(k)s, 401(a)s, 403(b)s, etc. With the exception of Roth-type retirement accounts, every dollar withdrawn from a retirement account is subject to ordinary income tax at the recipient's rate. With these types of accounts "stretching out" income tax deferred growth is often a goal of the taxpayer. Stretch-out strategies involve structuring the retirement account to keep the minimum required distribution as small as possible.

Keeping these assets in the family is also a challenge. This is because the only way to stretch out the retirement account when the spouse of the account owner is the intended beneficiary is to name the spouse as the beneficiary. When that happens, and it is often a good strategy, the surviving spouse can make the account his own. And he usually does. The stretch-out strategy can now work. The challenge comes when the surviving spouse names beneficiaries other than his deceased spouse's children.

The loss of the stretch out when passing qualified assets through a trust for the benefit of a surviving spouse is one of the reasons the surviving spouse is usually named as beneficiary of a retirement account. As noted, however, this strategy has its own risks. Income-tax deferral is not lost when a properly drafted trust created for the benefit of a non-spouse is the beneficiary of the retirement account.

Because of the income-tax liability associated with most retirement accounts, they are a favored asset to give to charities. Qualified charities do not pay income taxes and thus are as grateful receiving a $10,000 retirement account as they are when they receive a $10,000 check from your bank account.

What Benjamin Franklin said about death and taxes is still true. What has changed in our world is the emphasis from estate tax planning to income tax planning.

Of course, we hope you remember those 4 simple questions that will give you confidence that your plan is designed to protect your assets and to achieve your objects.

Can you still say YES to our four simple questions:

1. Do I understand my estate plan?
2. Does it meet my goals and will it have a positive impact on my beneficiaries?
3. Are my assets titled in a manner consistent with my plan?
4. Have I thoroughly informed my helpers of my wishes and kept them up-to-date on changes in my thinking and to my plan? (i.e. Do they know what I want them to do?)

Chapter 9: Title –
How You Own Your "Stuff"
and Why It Matters

Title, the way you own your assets, is critical to the success of your estate plan. Incorrect title is one of the most common reasons estate plans do not work as intended. Title controls the distribution of your assets. In this chapter we will describe some common ways people own their assets and how that may affect their estate plan. How you own your "stuff" really does matter and we will explain why.

There are several ways to transfer assets to your beneficiaries. Each depends on how the asset is owned. Generally speaking, if you have a will-based plan and you want your will to control your assets at death, your assets will be titled in your name alone. While if you have a trust-based plan, you will transfer your assets to the trustee of your trust (usually you), allowing you to avoid probate.

Joint Tenancy

For married couples, the most common form of transferring assets from one spouse to another is through the use of joint ownership – formally referred to as joint tenancy with right of survivorship, or joint tenancy for short. Sometimes joint tenancy between spouses is the correct form of ownership; sometimes it is not.

You do not have to be married to own an asset jointly with another person. In fact, you may own an asset jointly with more than one other person. The way joint tenancy operates is when one of the joint tenants dies, the remaining joint tenant (or tenants) now owns the deceased person's interest in the property.

Joint tenancy can be very effective planning tool. It can also lead to unintended consequences and disrupt your plan, so be careful. A couple of stories can help illustrate a few of the common misconceptions and risks associated with joint tenancy.

Years ago we were reviewing a new client's Personal Information Form. We noticed he had two $50,000 CDs, each jointly titled with a friend of his – one with Bob and the other with Bill. We commented on our client's generosity and how he must be really fond of Bob and Bill. Our client replied excitedly: "Yes, and look here in my Will. See, I have included these gifts, one for Bob and one for Bill."

He was right, upon reviewing his will, we saw it said: "I specifically bequeath $50,000 to Bob and $50,000 to Bill."

We then commented he was even more generous than we had originally thought, his plan included gifts to Bob and Bill in the amount $100,000 each. Agitated our client responded "No, no, $50,000 only, $50,000 each." He thought that he was describing the gift of the CD in his will, not making an additional gift.

In what we had hoped was a kind response, we replied: "Well actually, that's not quite right. You are giving them each $100,000. Your $50,000 CDs will be transferred to Bob and Bill immediately upon your death, and later, when your will is admitted to probate, the first gifts to be made after paying debts and expenses will be the specific $50,000 gifts to Bob and Bill."

Our client was not happy. Actually, he was furious. This was not what he intended. It took several minutes to carefully explain how joint tenancy operates.

Joint tenancy trumps the terms of a will.

Joint tenancy trumps the terms of a trust.

The surviving joint tenant(s) owns the property at the death of a joint tenant. Joint tenancy operates independently of a will or a trust, neither of those planning tools have anything to do with jointly titled property.

Another example of joint tenancy gone wrong involved a recently widowed woman who owned the family farm by reason of her late husband's death. Happy with the way joint tenancy had operated at her husband's death (no lawyers, no probate), she went to her lawyer's office and asked him to prepare a deed to transfer the farm to her and her only child as joint tenants with right of survivorship. She figured it worked well when her husband died, it would work well when she died.

A few years later something happened she never thought would happen again: she fell in love and remarried. Her new spouse lived on the other side of the country, and they decided to move there. She put the farm on the market, found a buyer and contacted her son to ask him to come to the closing to sign the deed. The son replied: "Oh yes, Mom. I will be there. When is it?"

And sure enough the son was there, and he signed the deed. What his mother didn't expect was he would be asking for, and receiving, one half of the proceeds from the sale. His mother had gifted him one half of the farm. Mother was not amused, nor had she expected this would be the result of creating a joint tenancy between herself and her son. Needless to say, the parent/child relationship deteriorated that day.

The lesson here is when the mother placed the farm in her name and the name of her child as joint tenants she made a gift to her son of a half interest in the farm.

Another possible risk of joint tenancy, especially with a non-spouse, occurs when mom or dad dies. The jointly titled asset will go directly to the surviving tenant, typically a child. What happens if mom or dad had more than one child? Will the child who is a surviving joint tenant divide the account among her siblings, or will she keep it for herself? The law does not require division.

And yet another risk of joint tenancy with a non-spouse is if the non-spouse joint tenant is sued. The most common suit for married people is divorce. In the case with the mother mentioned above, would the farm be subject to the terms of her child's divorce? This is a question we would rather not have to address.

Our rule of thumb is do not create joint tenancy with a non-spouse unless the asset is of a modest value that will not negatively impact your life or estate plan if lost.

Tenants in Common

Tenants in Common is similar to joint tenancy in that two or more people have an interest in the same thing, but the result of one of the tenant's death is different: his interest in the property will be distributed according to the terms of his will or trust. It does not automatically vest with the surviving tenant(s) at death.

Transfer on Death

Another form of ownership is what we refer to as transfer-on-death assets ("TOD"). Perhaps the most common form of this type of asset is a life insurance policy or a retirement account.

Both of these types of assets are contracts which require you to name a beneficiary and an alternate beneficiary. Failure to name a beneficiary for an asset controlled by beneficiary designation results in the asset being owned by your estate at your death. This is rarely a good result. It can lead to unwanted probate administration and it may end up with the wrong beneficiaries or expose otherwise protected assets to creditors.

As with a will or a trust, there are three possible beneficiaries of an asset controlled by beneficiary designations: individuals, trusts, or charities. As previously noted, if you have a retirement plan and charities you wish to benefit at your death, naming charities as a beneficiary of a retirement plan is a very income-tax efficient way of satisfying charitable bequests. This is because charities do not pay income taxes, while individual beneficiaries do and every dollar of a retirement plan is taxed, except for Roth type plans.

In addition to retirement plans and life insurance policies, some financial institutions permit pay-on-death (POD) or transfer-on-death (TOD) titling for bank accounts and even investment accounts. In our experience, institutions offering this form of ownership are inconsistent in their rules with respect to how many beneficiaries can be named and what type of account can use this form of asset ownership and asset transfer.

Trustee owned Assets

If assets are owned by a revocable trust and you are the trustmaker and the trustee, you may use the trust assets in any manner you wish. If someone other than the trustmaker is the trustee, then the assets owned by the trust will be managed and distributed according to the terms of the trust.

For trust-based plans it is important to transfer your assets to the trust. And sometimes name the trust as the beneficiary of assets controlled by beneficiary designations.

Title Trumps Your Will and Trust

As you may now realize, there are several options for how you own your assets. Each titling method offers certain features that may or may not work well with your needs and situation. The important thing to realize is how you own your stuff really does matter. An adage that we often share with clients is Title Trumps Documents.

You also need to be clear on who controls the assets under each type of ownership now, during your incapacity, and after your death. The chart below, set up as a mini quiz, may help you map out who controls what on your behalf:

Joint Tenancy	In My Own Name	In Trust	Beneficiary Designation
Now (Who controls?)	Now (Who controls?)	Now (Who controls?)	Now (Who controls?)
Upon Incapacity (Who controls?)	Upon Incapacity (Who controls?)	Upon Incapacity (Who controls?)	Upon Incapacity (Who controls?)
After Death (Who controls?)	After Death (Who controls?)	After Death (Who controls?)	After Death (Who controls?)

Once you have designed and created your plan, it is critical to go through your estate, asset by asset and make sure each is titled in a manner consistent with the terms of your plan. Please do not ignore some assets because "they aren't worth much." Decisions based on this type of thinking have caused heartache and wasted time for helpers, including unnecessary probate and lost assets. Take your spouse out to dinner with that small nest egg or close the account and combine it with another account, just don't leave it and forget about it.

By now, you are probably already asking yourself our four simple questions:

1. Do I understand my estate plan?
2. Does it meet my goals and will it have a positive impact on my beneficiaries?

3. Are my assets titled in a manner consistent with my plan?
4. Have I thoroughly informed my helpers of my wishes and kept them up-to-date on changes in my thinking and to my plan? (i.e. Do they know what I want them to do?)

Chapter 10:
Your "Other" Legacy

In the end, we are all more than our balance sheet. Yet this important part, our story or legacy, is often overlooked and forgotten. We frequently spend too little time, or no time at all, thinking about that other, key part of our legacy. How will we be remembered? Sometimes our only written legacy is what appears as an obituary in a local paper. If that is all that remains, what do you want it to say?

Many of our clients have found that by writing their own obituary or life account, they are leaving a legacy that goes beyond the distribution of assets. Capturing details of our stories while we're still alive gives us the opportunity to say, "These parts of my life were important to me." Thinking about our other, non-financial legacy can in-fluence our decisions regarding the disbursement of financial assets to our beneficiaries. It can help us focus on core val-ues, philosophy and stewardship.

The process of writing your obituary can fill an important role in recording your life. In the end, it may serve as one of the most important gifts you leave behind.

As we prepare trusts, wills, and advance directives to of-fer guidance to our families and friends when the end of life arrives, we often spend too little time thinking about that key part of our legacy. How will we be remembered? Sometimes a written legacy is what appears as an obituary in a local paper. If that is all that remains, what do you want it to say? Who are you?

On the surface, this question seems simple. We know who we are and so do those nearest and dearest to us. Experience, however, teaches us the reality is far more complex. Our own memories may not match those of the people with whom we have lived for years, let alone the recollections of those, such as children, who lived in our houses while growing up, but now have their own lives, possibly many miles away. The events and character traits we think define our lives may not be the first things others think of when they think of us.

Who best knows us? We do. Usually the most precise information available for an obituary was written by the subject as a book-length memoir, a shorter biographical essay, entries in diaries or journals, letters, or contributions to class histories for college or high school. Nowadays, technology allows more people to record their memories as videos that can be posted on Internet websites such as YouTube. Even with the increased ease and variety of mediums to record our story, how many of us take the time to do so?

Bryan Marquard, the editor of the Obituaries Pages at the Boston Globe for the last 19 years suggests finding a way to capture the first-person account of a life and experience will help engage readers, family, friends and acquaintances. Something as simple as an updated resume is invaluable to an obituary writer.

Mr. Marquard goes on to say "We may think relatives remember when we changed jobs or changed addresses, and surely they remember where we went to school and what year we married. Many of us would be surprised to learn how many such details are remembered in a fuzzy fashion, if they are remembered at all, after we're gone." In fact, Mr. Marquard continues, "The question children most often stumble on when I'm writing an obituary about their parents is: What year did they marry? And these are ostensibly the easiest details to remember. A resume can list graduation years and a college major, but it offers no clue about whether you liked or hated college, and how the experience shaped you."

Why should we prepare a record our lives? Doing so helps us shape our "other" legacy, the one that goes beyond disbursement of assets. Capturing details of our lives while we're still alive gives us the opportunity to say, "These parts of my life were important to me."

How do we go about preparing such records? There are many sites on the Internet, including for-profit businesses. Below are links to three sites that offer advice and, in some cases charge a fee. We advise that you not pay for a service, but simply review some suggestions these sites offer, and go over the questions they post as prompts for how you can go about sharing your other legacy. The final link is to a paid death notice that is an example of how one person, or his family, captured his rather unusual life.

http://www.therememberingsite.org/view.php
The Remembering Site charges a fee for publishing an autobiography, but the site includes free links to scores of questions that make people think about the details of their lives. These can address anwhere from listing family members to recalling details about where you grew up, where you went to school, what traditions you and your family held dear on holidays. Few will have the patience to go through all the questions and write long answers to each, but looking at the list is a good exercise in establishing recollections.

http://obituaryguide.com/writeyourown.php

Obituary Guide begins by briefly discussing practical and legal matters, such as health care directives and powers of attorney.The tone shifts, however, from your paperwork to listing the facts of your life. It encourages a focus on anecdotes and recollections. As previously noted, the milestone dates of your life are essential; what they mean is more important.

http://www.livewelldogood.com/memoir-writing.php

Live Well, Do Good offers 10 tips, among them that the first step is simply beginning to write out your ideas. Sentences and paragraphs can be rewritten and improved, but first they must be written. Another tip is to write for yourself, rather than thinking about what others will think. Those who encounter writer's block face few hurdles more challenging than being paralyzed by the thought of other eyes reading what you write. Think first about your own eyes.

An Internet cottage industry of sorts is emerging among people who write their own paid death notices, or family members who help them do so, and everyone seems to be trying to come up with the description that is most likely to become an Internet sensation. We are sure some of them are somewhat or mostly true. Here is the beginning of one that recently made the rounds of web sites:

William Freddie McCullough - The man. The myth. The legend. Men wanted to be him and women wanted to be with him. William Freddie McCullough died on September 11, 2013. Freddie loved deep fried Southern food smothered in Cane Syrup, fishing at Santee Cooper Lake, Little Debbie Cakes, Two and a Half Men, beautiful women, Reese's Cups and Jim Beam. Not necessarily in that order. He hated vegetables and hypocrites. Not necessarily in that order.

Chapter 11:
Maintaining Your Plan –
Things Happen

Estate plans come in many shapes and sizes. Effective plans have one thing in common: they work. However, getting to this point is a process. We regularly hear "Oh, estate planning, I've done that. My spouse and I did that ages ago." This approach may or may not work. Why leave it to chance?

As we have discussed throughout this book, creating a plan that works for you is one thing, keeping the plan and everyone involved up-to-date is another challenge.

It is a rare person who creates a plan and years later can answer YES to each of our four simple questions. Not because they are difficult or tricky questions, but because we forget, circumstances change and stuff happens. So here they are again:

1. Do I understand my estate plan?
2. Does it meet my goals and will it have a positive impact on my beneficiaries?
3. Are my assets titled in a manner consistent with my plan?
4. Have I thoroughly informed my helpers of my wishes and kept them up-to-date on changes in my thinking and to my plan? (i.e. Do they know what I want them to do?)

It is almost certain that anyone reading this book will experience one or more of the following (possibly multiple times) before they lose capacity or die:

- Changes in your personal situation
- Changes in your financial situation
- Changes in the legal environment (For example: Medicaid or tax rules change)
- Changes in your beneficiaries' situations
- Changes in your attorney's experience in drafting and settling estate plans
- Changes in your experience, your beneficiaries' circumstance, and in your thinking in general.

How will these changes impact your planning? It is impossible to know. All we can say is once you decide to create a plan, commit to a process to maintain it and adjust it as needed so that you can always answer YES to our 4 simple questions.

We offer our clients two different ways to work with us. One is a Three-Step Strategy, we call it Lifeplan™, sometimes referred to as the "we call you" planning process; the other is the Two-Step Strategy, we call it the Traditional planning process or the "you call us" planning process.

Lifeplan™: We call you to help you keep your plan up-to-date

We work together to develop a plan that meets your expectations and achieves your goals.

We assist you with titling all of your assets in a manner consistent with your planning goals.

We commit to a continuing education and improvement program to keep your plan updated, your assets properly titled, and you and your Helpers educated.

You commit to showing up and actively engaging in your planning.

Finally, we provide appropriate assistance for you and your Helpers to help you and your family through the transitions of life.

Traditional: You call us when you want to review and update your plan.

We work together to develop a plan that meets your expectations and achieves your goals.

You title all of your assets in a manner consistent with your planning goals.

You develop a process to keep your plan updated, your assets properly titled, and you and your Helpers educated.

And finally, if requested, we will provide appropriate assistance for you and your Helpers to help you and your family through the transitions of life.

What to do next:

Regardless of what you have done to build your plan in the past, it is always a good idea to review and evaluate. By now you may realize just how easy it can be to have a plan that no longer reflects your wishes or the changes in your life or the changes in your beneficiaries' lives.

We can help you clarify what your plan needs to do to reflect your needs, wishes, and preferences and then help you to build or revise your plan to increase the likelihood your plan will be effective.

It all starts with a conversation. We can help you get to those 4 important YES answers so you can be confident your plan will take care of you and take care of tomorrow

Call our office to schedule an Appointment:
Phone: **(603) 643-7577**
Toll Free: **(877) 643-7577**

Glossary

Administration/Settlement
The process by which assets in the name of a **decedent** are legally transferred to the decedent's heirs or beneficiaries. Administration can either be through a trust or by will.

Advance Directive
Includes a "Health Care Power of Attorney" and "Living Will." See below. A document designating persons to make health care decisions for you if you are unable to do so.

Annual Exclusion
The exclusion from gift taxes for gifts by each donor to each donee which is available on an annual basis. The annual exclusion is currently $15,000 per donor, per donee, per calendar year (indexed for inflation).

Attorney-in-Fact
A person named as an agent in a power of attorney.

Beneficiary
A person who is, or will be, a recipient of benefits from a will, an estate or a trust.

Bequest
A gift of property made in a will or trust.

Decedent
A person who has died.

Fiduciary
A person or corporation that occupies a position of trust and accountability. One who acts on behalf of another.

Funding/Asset Alignment

The process of transferring ownership or title of a person's assets in a manner that is consistent with their estate plan. This includes transferring assets to a Trustee of a trust, changing beneficiary designations and assigning interests in property.

Gift

A gratuitous transfer of property to someone else without receiving adequate consideration in return.

Grantor

The person who creates a trust (also known as trustor, settlor or trustmaker).

Guardianship

A probate court proceeding in which the judge considers whether a person has become so incapacitated that s/he needs someone else to make health care and financial decisions for her or him.

Intestate

When one dies without a valid estate plan, or where an estate plan does not dispose of all the decedent's property.

Joint Tenancy with Rights of Survivorship

A form of ownership of property among persons generally characterized by equality of ownership share and created at the same time. As an owner dies that person's interest is terminated and the last survivor(s) owns the entire title.

Living Probate

A judicial proceeding designed to protect an incapacitated person's well-being and property under the authority of the probate court.

Living Trust
A trust created by agreement currently, as opposed to a testamentary trust created by a Will. Such a trust can be used to hold assets during a person's lifetime and thereby remove those assets from probate at the person's incapacity or death. Also sometimes called an *inter vivos trust.*

Minimum Required Distribution
In most retirement accounts, sometimes referred to as qualified plans, the owner is required to begin making withdrawals from the account in the year after he or she reaches age 70 ½. These withdrawals must meet certain minimum distribution requirements. In general, the account owner must withdraw the funds over his or her life expectancy (if not more rapidly).

Personal Property
Tangible personal property means anything moveable that you can touch. Intangible personal property refers to financial assets such as stocks, bonds, bank accounts, insurance, etc.

Personal Representative
A personal representative is a catch-all term that includes all manner of fiduciary, including agents, trustees, executors and administrators.

P.O.D./T.O.D
An instruction to a depository institution, such as a bank, to pay the funds in the account to the beneficiary named in the memorandum signed by the account owner at the owner's death.

Pour-over Will
A will which names the Trustee of an existing trust as the principal beneficiary. Thus, the probate estate "pours over" into the trust estate.

Power of Attorney
A grant of power to a person (agent) to make or carry out the decisions of the signer of the document (principal), which expires upon the death of the principal. A durable power document continues in effect during the principal's incapacity if it contains specific language required by state law.

Probate
The process of administrating a decedent's estate under the authority of the probate court.

Property
Anything owned by a person or entity. Property is divided into two types: "real property," which is any interest in land, real estate, and "personal property" (sometimes called "personalty"), which is all other property.

Qualified Plan Assets
Property held in an I.R.A., 401(k), 403(b), or other pension plan on which the owner has not yet paid federal income tax; sometimes called tax-deferred.

Real Property
Land, and anything permanently attached to it, such as a house.

Remainderman
The persons who will receive the benefit from a trust after the death of the income beneficiary(ies).

Residuary
The clause in a trust or will that disposed of all of the decedent's property not previously mentioned. This clause usually begins, "All the rest, residue and remainder of my property, of whatsoever kind and nature, and wherever situated, I give..."

Testator

The person who creates and signs the will.

Trust

Instructions for the use of property over a period of time, often measured by lives. There are two primary reasons to create a trust: one concerns process, it is generally easier to manage assets during incapacity and following death if all of a person's assets are in trust. The second concerns substance, a trust can provide asset protection for the beneficiaries of the trust. A trust has a trustmaker, a trustee, and beneficiaries. The trust defines the trustee's powers and duties and the beneficiaries' rights, if any.

Trusts may be revocable (the trustmaker may amend or revoke the trust instrument) or irrevocable (neither the trustmaker nor the beneficiaries of the trust may revoke the trust).

Trustee

A person or corporation appointed by the trustmaker to take control of trust property and administer it for the benefit of the beneficiaries of the trust.

Will

A document (testament) executed by a testator which sets out the testator's instructions for winding up his or her affairs and disposing of assets after death. The will has no effect until the testator dies.

About the Authors

Timothy W. Caldwell, Counselor at Law, has 28 years of experience in the Upper Valley and since 1997, has concentrated his practice on estate planning and settlement. He graduated cum laude from Dartmouth College and earned his Juris Doctorate from Georgetown University Law Center. He served as chair and member of the Lyme School Board, the Upper Valley Planned  Giving Council, and currently serves on the Upper Valley Regional Advisory Board to the New Hampshire Charitable Foundation. Tim was instrumental in establishing LeaveALegacy®NH/VT.

Prior to practicing law, Tim was a competitive cross country skier. He competed in four Olympics and three World Championships. His wife, Margaret, is a long-time Social Studies teacher at Hanover High School. They have three children, Lucy (Papault), Heidi and Patrick. Margaret and Tim have lived in Lyme Center, New Hampshire, since 1989.

Renée A. Harvey, Counselor at Law, has worked in the New York,Vermont and New Hampshire legal systems since 1990. She is a graduate of Vermont Law School and is licensed to practice law in the state and federal courts of  New Hampshire and Vermont. Her practice focuses on estate planning, settlement,and assisting clients in making informed decisions. She is a Respecting Choices® Advance Care Planning Certified Facilitator and a certified mediator. Renée also serves on the New Hampshire BarAssociation's Dispute Resolution Committee, the Patient Choices Vermont Advisory Committee, and as a lecturer at various local institutions. She is a managing partner at Caldwell Law

Meet Our Team

Top Row left to right: Attorney Timothy Caldwell, Julie Cryans, Sheila Smith, Dina D'cruze, Jaclyn Hatt, Joanne Oscadal, Attorney Renée Harvey, Attorney James Thaxton
Bottom Row left to right: Deb Eaton and Linda Lagasse
Missing: Pam Lain, Andrew Hammond

Caldwell Law

Hanover Road Professional Center
367 Route 120, Suite B-6, Lebanon NH 03766 **Phone: (603) 643-7577 Toll Free: (877) 643-7577 estateandelderlawgroup.com**

Reference Notes